Noah is busy sawing wood.
What is he making?
Join up the dots to find out.

Abraham is leaving his home in Ur.
He is going to a new land.
Help him find the right road.

Jacob gave his son Joseph a present.
It was a wonderful new coat.
Use your felt-tips to finish the picture.

Moses is in the desert.
He sees a bush on fire.
Join the dots to finish the picture.

Ruth is collecting wheat.
Two bundles of wheat are exactly the same.
Can you find them?

Samuel is helping in God's Temple.
He is lighting the candles.
Join the dots to finish the drawing.

Jesus is twelve years old.
Mary and Joseph are
taking him to Jerusalem.
Which road must
they follow?

Jesus is at a wedding party.
He turns water into wine!
Circle the two wine jars that
are exactly the same.

Here are Jesus' special friends.
How many are there?
Trace over the numbers.

Jesus has come to the river.
John is baptizing him there.
Use crayons or felt-tips to finish the picture.

Jesus is beside the sea.
He helps his friends catch lots of fish.
Use your felt-tips to finish the picture.

Jesus is going to visit Mary and Martha. Which road must he take?